A Life of Praise

By

Jacki K. Work

PublishAmerica
Baltimore

© 2005 by Jacki K. Work.
All rights reserved. No part of this book may be reproduced, stored in a retrieval system or transmitted in any form or by any means without the prior written permission of the publishers, except by a reviewer who may quote brief passages in a review to be printed in a newspaper, magazine or journal.

First printing

ISBN: 1-4137-6690-0
PUBLISHED BY PUBLISHAMERICA, LLLP
www.publishamerica.com
Baltimore

Printed in the United States of America

Contents

Acknowledgments	5
Introduction	7
Week One: Praise 101	9
What Causes Praise?	12
Pain and Suffering	14
Self Praise	17
False Praise	20
Promised Praise	22
Christian Praise	25
Week Two: Honor	27
Teaching Honor	29
Honor Through Giving	31
Honor in Receiving	33
Honor Through Discipline	35
Honor Through Prayer	37
Christian Life of Praise Through Honor	39
Week Three: Praise Through Worship	40
Worship in Reverence	42
Worship Through Expressed Reverence	44
Worship in Devotion	46
Worship in Song	48
Worship in Spirit and Truth	51
Worship in the Beauty of Holiness	53

Week Four: Praise Through Prayer	55
Prayer Commitment	57
Pray – To Whom?	59
Pray in Faith	61
Pray for Others	63
Pray for Healing	65
Living in the Power of Prayer	67
Week Five: Love	68
Accepting the Embrace	70
Understanding the Embrace	71
His Embrace Through Service	73
Returning the Embrace	76
Accepting the Territory	77
Praise – the Lifestyle of Jesus	79
Psalm 23	81
Study/Discussion Notes	82
Bibliography	84

Acknowledgments

With more than 40 years of affiliation with The Salvation Army and 15 years at the Orchard United Methodist Church in Farmington Hills, Michigan, I will not attempt to list the many leaders and friends to whom I am indebted for their spiritual influence on my life. I simply say THANK YOU!

A special thanks for the input and support of my adult Bible discussion class.

Finally, this study would not exist without the loving, persistent encouragement of my sister, Pamela Mack.

I dedicate this study to you,
Pam

Introduction

"I will sing of your steadfast love, O Lord forever; with my mouth I will proclaim your faithfulness to all generations" (Psalm 89: 1).

What does the word praise bring to mind? To most people it is centered around a good deed or series of good deeds that result in one or more goals being accomplished. In the pages that follow we will look at praise through the lifestyle and teachings of Jesus Christ. A praise that resulted in good works coming from a heart of love.

If you are using this book for an adult study class, you will find questions relating to each week's study in the back of the book. Instruct the class to take a moment before each day's study to praise God.

I do not consider myself to be a great theologian or scholar, yet God has led me to write this short study on praise. Thus, I pick up the towel of service and carry my cross in obedience as a humble servant of Christ.

"Through Him then, let us continually offer a sacrifice of praise to God that is, the fruit of our lips that confess His name. Do not neglect to do good and to share what you have" (Hebrews 13: 15a).

Week One
Praise 101

Jesus taught and lived a life of praise to God, our Father. His childhood found him in the temple where he learned about the Holy Law from the elders. He then continued in a consistent life of praise to God through his giving, discipline, prayer, reverence, commitment, service, obedience and above all, praise in submission. *"Not what I will but as you will and desire"* (Matthew 26: 39b AMP).

> *"In Him you also, when you heard the word of truth, the gospel of your salvation, and believed in Him, were marked with the seal of the promised Holy Spirit; this is the pledge of our inheritance toward redemption as God's people, to the praise of His glory"* (Ephesians 1: 13-14).

PRAISE: The dictionary definition of praise is "to express approval of." This is an active praise of approval of something passed. Praise also holds an expectation of the future as when we praise a child or give praise at work There is an unspoken expectation that the child will continue in good behavior or the employee will continue in good work performance. When we offer praise to God, there is an unspoken expectation that God will continue his love and guidance. In general, our praise is for all good things. Where then is our praise in times of trial?

> *"In this you rejoice, even if now for a little while you have had to suffer various trials, so that the genuineness of your faith, being more precious than gold that, though perishable,*

is tested by fire, may be found to result in praise and glory and honor when Jesus Christ is revealed" (I Peter 1: 6-7).

"SUFFER VARIOUS TRIALS...TESTED BY FIRE" If we knew in advance what life holds for us, the suffering and sorrow, would we continue to praise God? What if we knew that tomorrow we would lose a loved one to an unexpected death or that we would be diagnosed with a terminal illness? Would we continue to praise God and express approval of his love? For many believers, praise to God is determined by the outcome of an event or happening in their life. It is, as the dictionary states, an "approval of," which implies something of the past. Thank God that the dictionary is not the final word. To the believer, the Bible is the final word. It is the word of past, present and future. By its truths our unspoken expectations become praise in anticipation for eternal life with our Father. The simple prayer that Jesus taught the disciples is a great example of praise in anticipation of the future.

"Our Father, which art in Heaven
hallowed be thy name.
Thy Kingdom come, thy will be done,
on earth as it is in Heaven.
Give us this day our daily bread,
and forgive us our trespasses,
as we forgive those who trespass against us.
And lead us not into temptation
but deliver us from evil" (Matthew 6: 9-13 KJV).

The roots of this prayer are firmly planted in the experience of the past and present and it thrives on the anticipation of the future. We too can praise God in anticipation of love even through sickness and sorrow, suffering of trials and testing by fire. The key is in our faith that God is with us always. As the song writer, Stanley Ditmer, wrote, "What e're the future holds, I'm in His hands."

Take a moment to praise God for today and all of the tomorrows. Praise Him for his unconditional love and power of endurance in all things. His is the Kingdom and the power and the glory now and forever. AMEN!

Compliment God three times each day.

Week One - Day Two
What Causes Praise?

Praise usually follows good works or the fulfillment of expectation. The point of today's study will not be on the actual words spoken in praise. Today we will think about the honest cause of praise.

Praise can be words that have little or no meaning, like in a con game, rather than words of truth. These are words that are carefully disguised into phrases of kindness to seek control by manipulation. They are not from a heart of love but from a mind of greed.

What causes praise? Do we praise to manipulate others to our way of thinking, or is our praise from a loving heart that seeks to encourage others to think and walk their own predestined path with God? The Psalmist clearly rebuked those who praise deceitfully. *"You give your mouth free rein for evil, and your tongue frames deceit...but I now rebuke you..."* (Psalm 50: 19, 21b).

List below times in your life when you either received praise or gave praise for a job well done or an answer to prayer.

Received Praise   Gave Praise

1.   1.

2.   2.

3.   3.

Look at your list and think about how the praise was given. Was it given with an honest love?

It should be noted at the beginning of this study that praise for a job well done could create a negative situation. For example, we could be instilling in the minds of others the idea that praise is only given for a "job well done" and anything less is a failure. Praise, in this study, will include praise before, during and after any event. Thus, when giving praise to others, our praise would include an encouraging acknowledgment of the effort with further encouragement to continue in a path of righteousness.

There have been many times when I started a project with 110% enthusiasm only to have the project fail. Currently I am in charge of the senior citizen programming at our church. I started this program with my usual 110% enthusiasm and scheduled to take the seniors to see a play. I called the theater in advance to ask if the play would be appropriate for seniors from a church. I was told, "There is a small part in one scene that has a little rough language." Thinking that the seniors would not be offended by a "little rough language," I purchased the tickets. It turned out to be true; there were only a few rough words in one scene. However, in *every scene* one or more of the actors stripped to their underwear.

Was I praised for a job well done? To my surprise I was praised. The seniors were so concerned that I would be discouraged that they surrounded me with love and understanding. As we continue our study about praise, keep in mind that the emphasis is on the LOVE that causes praise.

What causes praise? To the believer, the salvation of God and praise are one and inseparable. If we walk with God we walk in praise to God and God lives in praise through our life. The "expressed approval" of our Father is found in the life, death and resurrection of Jesus Christ. It is our faith in God the Father and in the Godhood of Jesus Christ that not only causes praise but is praise in the highest.

Week One - Day Three
Praise Through Pain and Suffering

To suffer is to "feel pain, to bear loss, damage or injury." In addition, to suffer is to "endure, abide, tolerate, stand" (Merriam-Webster Dictionary). While suffering is indeed a time for pain, both mental and physical, it is also a time of endurance. To endure a test of faith through physical or emotional suffering is a positive action that leads to spiritual growth.

> *"For your sake we are being killed all day long; we are accounted as sheep to be slaughtered. No, in all these things we are more than conquerors through Him that loved us. For I am convinced that neither death, nor life, nor angels, nor rulers, nor things present, nor things to come, nor powers, nor height, nor depth, nor anything else in all creation, will be able to separate us from the love of God in Christ Jesus our Lord"* (Romans 8: 36-39).

Is there a person in your life who remains in their suffering almost saint-like? I recently watched a short news story about Chinese Christians who are living in communist China. They do not have the freedom of Christian worship and so they have organized underground churches and schools to study the Bible and lift their praise to God. What is it that strengthens these Christians? How can they utter words of praise through pain and loss? In the first chapter of James we find encouragement for times of pain and suffering. He writes:

"My brothers and sisters, whenever you face trials of any kind, consider it nothing but joy, because you know that the testing of your faith produces endurance; and let endurance have its full effect, so that you may be mature and complete, lacking in nothing" (James 1: 2-4).

We are human and a very real part of our humanity is weakness. Even Jesus was not exempt from loss, pain and moments of weakness. Jesus wept with the same human emotion that we experience. He cried, *"My God, my God, why hast thou forsaken me?"* Then by the power within he endured the pain and weakness to the point of submission to God's love and said, *"Not what I will, but as you will and desire."*

Can we praise God in suffering? Yes! Let me tell you a story about a 15-year-old girl who went with her pastor to visit an elderly couple, Mr. and Mrs. Baker, who lived in a state-subsidized project area. This church believed that it was good training for young people to visit shut-ins. As the girl entered the little apartment, she noticed immediately how dim it was. There was one small lamp on an end table attempting to light the living room area. In the bedroom the only light was from a small window, which obviously had not been cleaned for sometime. Mrs. Baker was in bed and looked very ill. The pastor talked with her for a short time and then turned to Mr. Baker and suggested that they find a phone to call the Baker's son. There was no phone in the apartment and cell-phones had not yet been invented, so the pastor asked the girl to stay with Mrs. Baker while he and Mr. Baker went out to find a phone. The girl pulled a chair next to the bed and sat there watching Mrs. Baker's chest move up and down in shallow breaths that were hardly audible. She was afraid. *What if Mrs. Baker dies while the pastor is gone?* she thought. Suddenly, Mrs. Baker's hand flopped toward her. Instinctively she reached for her hand which felt cold and lifeless. But as she looked at Mrs. Baker she thought she saw a smile in her eyes. Then, in a whisper of a voice, Mrs. Baker said, "God is good, isn't He." With that Mrs. Baker pulled her hand away and continued in her belabored breathing.

The young, 15-year-old girl was me and this experience will stay with me until the day I die. Here was an old lady, obviously weak from age and painfully aware of impending death, yet she felt compelled to praise God.

We need only look at the life of Jesus or Job or *(you fill in the name)* to see how love for the Father produces a fullness of endurance through pain and suffering, which is constantly trying to pull our thoughts inward and have us dwell on weakness. Their faith, confidence in the power of God, empowered them with endurance as a natural part of their human/spiritual experience.

Take a moment and look back at your life. Think of the times of pain and suffering when God has given you the power to endure. For those of you who are at this moment in pain and suffering, be assured that endurance is a gift of the Spirit. God will not allow any suffering or pain beyond your endurance, more importantly, His endurance through you. Remember the words of James, *"Let endurance have its full effect,"* so that *" you may be mature and complete, lacking in nothing."*

Week One– Day Four
Self Praise

"Do not love the world or the things in the world. The love of the Father is not in those who love the world; for all that is in the world—the desire of the flesh, the desire of the eyes, the pride of riches—comes not from the Father but from the world. And the world and its desire are passing away, but those who do the will of God live forever" (I John 2: 15-17).

Believers working at home or away from home seek to do their very best. They attack each day seeking to accomplish good things. The result is the satisfaction of a day well spent. Nonbelievers also attack each day seeking to do their best. So where is the difference between the believer and the nonbeliever? The difference is in two parts. *First,* there is belief in the supreme authority of God. The nonbeliever's desire for each day is to prove himself superior. He will strive to position himself above others and will maneuver to place himself with people of authority or popularity, believing that all good is self-made. For the believer, the desire to give time, talent and energy toward advancement is basically the same as the nonbeliever, but there is one major difference. To the believer God is the supreme authority who directs his life. He does not believe that all good is self-made but gives all praise to God. He believes in the very simple diagnosis of the Bible, which teaches that man either believes in himself as the supreme authority or he believes in the supreme authority of God.

The belief in the supreme authority, a higher power, is part of the various 12-step programs, which are so prevalent in our country. There is no argument from Christians, that Bill W., a cofounder of Alcoholics

Anonymous, was changed when he had a profound spiritual experience in which he realized, *Who am I to say there is no God?*. From that moment his understanding of God gave him the power to stay sober for the remainder of his life. The Alcoholics Anonymous program now has over 2 million members in its fellowship. One of the great lessons of this program is that self-centeredness must be destroyed in favor of all things being turned over to the "Father of light," the Great Power, the supreme authority of us all. I would add that the Great Power has a name; it is God. Belief in the supreme authority of God has and continues to change the lives of millions of people throughout the world. The beauty of this change is that their witness will cause others to follow. The greatest example of this truth is found in the life of Jesus.

Second, the actions of our belief. To the believer, the desire for personal recognition is joined with God's Spirit. He desires all of his activities to be recognized by others in a way that will give God the praise and glory. The nonbeliever desires his actions to result in praise for himself. His excuse for what he perceives to be failure is almost always found outside of himself. He blames the situations or other people for his failure. His success is determined by what he perceives to be wealth and authority. All praise and authority must be directed to him. This focus on self-praise is most harmful to those who are weak in nature. Their constant failure to meet self-imposed goals create a stress that can drive them to permanent mental and physical illness. The Spirit-filled Christian lives in praise with heart to God and hand to man.

List 3 Good Accomplishments in Your Life

1.

2.

3.

List 3 Events in Your Life Where You Experienced Failure to accomplish a specific goal.

1.

2.

3.

Look at the lists above and ask yourself if there was praise to God in both the accomplishments and the (perceived) failures.

Praise to God must be active and constant in *all* that life has to offer. It is this praise in the supreme authority of God and the actions of that belief which separates the Christian from self praise.

Here is a simple test: When you look into the mirror each morning, do you see an image that you created or the image of God's creation?

Week One – Day Five
False Praise

Human nature is such that a little praise will go a long way. Our response is a momentary satisfaction of self-worth that becomes a mini-foundation of confidence. But what if the praise is given from a heart of greed?

> *"Beware of false prophets, who come to you in sheep's clothing but inwardly are ravenous wolves. You will know them by their fruits"* (Matthew 7: 15-16a).

As a young adult, I worked in the accounting department of a major banking company in Detroit, Michigan. I have a gift for solving accounting problems, consequently, coworkers were constantly asking me for help in balancing their accounts. On one occasion, a coworker had a problem in accounts receivables and came to me for assistance. A few hours later the problem was solved and she praised me for my good work. The next day, in a meeting with management, I listened as my coworker explained how *she* had solved the problem. After the meeting I followed her to her office and shut the door. When our discussion was over, there was no doubt in her mind that I would no longer be available to assist her in solving any accounting problems. Manipulative as she was, she used my anger against me by telling management that I would not work with her due to some petty incident. In other words, she told them that I was not a team player. She was truly a wolf in sheep's clothing. I could leave the story right here and you might think that it is a fair illustration of false praise. But if you read the story again, you will discover that my reaction to her false praise allowed my anger, instead of love, to control my actions. Do you see how false praise and deception can, as savage wolves, destroy the flock?

> *"I know that after I have gone, savage wolves will come in among you, not sparing the flock. Some even from your own group will come distorting the truth in order to entice the disciples to follow them"* (Acts 20: 29-30).

Within our churches we find false praise, and why not? The spirit of evil (Satan) need not waste his time on evildoers who are already in his control. No, he wants complete control of the universe and all of its inhabitants. We need only watch one day of television to realize that the spirit of evil is in control of much of its programming. Unfortunately, thousands are being manipulated by its false teachings of the meaning of life. Where there is false teaching, you can be assured that false praise is not far behind.

Should we be wary of everyone we meet? Of course not, but we should be aware that false praise abounds. The Bible is clear about our actions as believers. We must, at all times, be truthful and honest, producing *"...The harvest of righteousness that comes through Jesus Christ for the glory and praise of God"* (Philippians 1:11).

Week One – Day Six
Promised Praise

STORY #1: A man in his early 50s was sailing on Lake Superior one bright Sunday afternoon. This was a much needed vacation from his job, which was not difficult but very demanding of his time. Most Sundays would find him in church, however, on this Sunday his thoughts were centered on the pleasures of sailing. *It doesn't get any better than this,* he thought, when suddenly a huge gust of wind hit the sail and caught him off guard. As he reached for the wheel, a large wave hit and he lost his balance. The jolt sent him in the opposite direction of the wheel. He was still on his feet but the momentum of his weight pulled him toward the side rail. He grabbed the rail but was unable to secure his footing, and overboard he went. The sun was now setting, and dark clouds were forming. He watched as his sailboat drifted farther and farther away. Land was in sight but the force of the waves was greater than the strength of his arms and legs to swim ashore. Trying to remain calm, he stopped swimming to see what would happen if he allowed the waves to take control of his direction. He was floating away from land and there were no other boats in sight. Alone and frightened, he remembered that he had not told anyone where he was going this weekend. In desperation he cried, *Oh God, if you will save me I promise to be more faithful. I will become more involved in your work and will praise you forever. Please God save me.*

STORY #2: An elderly lady was driving along on the highway when suddenly a deer ran in front of her car. In an instant she slammed on the brakes and steered the car to the side of the road. Unfortunately, she hit some soft gravel. The car skidded out of control, slid down an embankment and hit a tree. The lady was knocked unconscious. When she woke up, she tried to move but the pain in her legs and chest was too great. She was sure that death was eminent. *Lord*, she prayed, *if it be thy will that I die, please watch over my family. I put my life in your hands.*

In both of these stories we find praise to God. The sailor made a deal with God, *"If you save me, I promise I will be faithful."* This was a desperate promise of praise like playing a jukebox, he put in a coin (prayer) and selected his music (blessing). ***Selective prayer yields selective results.***

The elderly lady made no such deal with God. She prayed, *"If it be thy will."* Her praise was for the fulfillment of God's will for her life.

Are there any events where you have found yourself making promises to God in exchange for a blessing in return? List them below:

Human nature directs our thinking to the belief that all gifts given deserve gifts of equal value in return. With God, all blessings are one way—from God to mankind. Promised praises are idle talk to God. He hears what we promise and in return says, *"Dear child, my promise and my love are free. Live and trust in this truth."*

When we, in trust, accept the promise of God, we are led away from the limited thinking of *let's make a deal*. Trust leads us to a loving submission that prays, *Thy will be done*. Trust leads to spiritual wisdom. *"Trust in the Lord with all your heart, and do not rely on your own insight. In all your ways acknowledge Him, and He will make straight your paths"* (Proverbs 3: 5-6). When we trust in the Lord with all of our hearts, our thoughts turn from, *what I can give to God,* to receiving what *God has to give to us.* Our promised praise will then give way to His everlasting love working through our lives.

Week One – Day Seven
Christian Praise

To praise God does not mean that we must be a person of low self-esteem. God teaches us through his word that Christians are a people of CONFIDENCE (Proverbs 3:26), ENDURANCE (I Corinthians 13:7) and MORE THAN CONQUERORS (Romans 8:37). Every recorded word and action of Jesus teaches us the depth of his humanity and spirituality. His life was not a life of low self-esteem nor a life of self or false praise. Jesus taught us the "full effect" of the joy of endurance and anticipation. His life and death is not something of the past that is complete and finished because it continues in the resurrection where he lives today. Therefore, it is not the love behind our praise but the love in front of our praise that pleases God. Because His Spirit lives today we praise God in anticipation of the "full effect" of the joy of endurance.

List below your immediate thoughts about the above statements:

1.

2.

To praise God at the foot of the cross is good. To get stuck there will limit God's Spirit of love to work through our lives. We must turn our eyes away from the cross to see what Jesus saw before he took His last breath. He looked with compassion on a people in need who were caught up in the security of a hate-filled crowd full of self-praise. He also saw his family and other Christians filled with love. From this we learn that to follow Jesus we should look with compassion to the needs of others and accept the understanding and comfort of our Christian family. We must praise God for the cross, but always remember Jesus words, *"Do this."* Two words that carry us into today. He did not say, *What have you done to please me?* He said, *"Do this."* What does this mean? Simply to follow Jesus's example to honor, glorify, pray and live praise to God.

Christian praise is active anticipation, putting love in front of the praise and then putting our praise into action. *"Praise the Lord, all you nations! Extol Him, all you peoples! For great is His steadfast love toward us, and the faithfulness of the Lord endures forever, praise the Lord"* (Psalm 117).

Week Two – Day One
Honor

"...But now the Lord declares...for those who honor me I will honor, and those who despise me shall be treated with contempt" (I Samuel 2:30).

One of the ways to praise God is through honor. List below some ways in which you honor God:

1.

2.

3.

We know that our responsibility is first to God and we praise Him daily through reading His Word and through prayer. But the responsibility of honor through praise should not end at the last amen of our daily devotions. It must continue through His call for action to give respect to His omnipotence as the almighty authority of love. The Bible teaches us to *Honor thy father and mother; Do not hide your light under a bushel, let it shine for all to see; Honor the Lord with your substance*. These are ways to show respect which gives honor to God. The greatest teacher of all, Jesus Christ, taught a reverent submission that was designated by God to teach outward respect through honor.

Look at your list above. Without seeing your list, I venture to say that it is much like mine. We honor God through prayer, reading scripture, attending church, etc., etc. This is good, but in all that we do we must be careful that the satisfaction of self does not override the genuineness of our faith, which is to give all praise and glory and honor to God.

As you enter this second week of study about praise to God through honor, think about what honor means to you. *"...humility goes before honor"* (Proverbs 15:33).

Week Two - Day Two
Teaching Honor

At an early age we learn to use words such as *on my honor*, *I cross my heart* and *I promise*. Once these phrases of promise are spoken the person hearing them is expected to have faith in the character and truthfulness of the one who is giving the promise. To praise God through honor is to have faith in Jesus Christ and His words of promise. We then put our faith into action by being a living example of love and thus we teach others to honor God.

> *"Go therefore and make disciples of all nations, baptizing them in the name of the Father and of the Son and of the Holy Spirit, and teaching them to obey everything that I have commanded you. And remember, I am with you always, to the end of the age"* (Matthew 28:19).

Many will shy away from passages of scripture that use the word "teach." They think that teachers are those who have dedicated a portion of their life to study and knowledge and are somewhat an expert, an authority figure. I suspect that we all have a tendency to think of teachers in this way and so it is a little frightening when we read scripture passages that admonish us to teach. Perhaps it will ease our thoughts if we think of teaching as sharing. Sharing is a normal part of our life process. Each generation passes to the next its basic beliefs and this sharing of knowledge is teaching. Our life would be entirely different if previous generations had not shared their experiences of life.

The Holy Bible is a collection of inspired writings about the life experiences of men and women like you and me. We read the Bible to learn more of God's promises and how to apply them to our life but what do we do with this knowledged? Its influence on our life will continue only to the extent that we build on the basics of its truth and act on the age-old process of sharing. God gives to all of His children the gift of teaching through sharing. There may be some who are led to the profession of teaching, but all are commissioned to be teachers of His love.

The apostle Paul writes in II Timothy 2:2: *"What you have heard from me...entrust to faithful people who will be able to teach others as well."* Paul is suggesting that Christians teach Christians so that they, in turn, will teach others. Sounds simple enough, so why is it that many Christians are so eager to share the experiences of everyday events, but reluctant to share about God's love in their life? Could it be that their actions are to honor themselves rather than to honor God? Part of the answer is found in Hebrews 5:11- 6:20. I will not give you the answer here but rather challenge you to find it for yourself in these verses of scripture.

We praise God through honor by teaching others of God's promise. Do not be overly concerned about what you will say or how you should act. In faith, let God do the teaching through your life.

Week Two – Day Three
Honor Through Giving

Jesus said, *"...from everyone to whom much has been given, much will be required..."* (Luke 12:48). Write a short statement about what it means to praise and honor God through giving.

Paul, in his last words to the elders of the church in Ephesus, Acts 20:17-35, pointed out that by his example he taught always to support, love and give to all people as Jesus said, *It is more blessed to give than to receive.* Paul also said, *God loves a cheerful giver.* In point of fact, we give that which is ours to give from the provisions that God has entrusted to us as His servants. What then do we have to give? The obvious answer is food, clothing, shelter and money. Jesus taught us that in giving to those who appear to have the least, we honor God. Indeed, the giving of material things is just and good when the seed of our giving is planted by God. Let's expand that thought to say that the giving of material things is a by-product of the gifts of His Spirit which are contributing factors in our calling as His disciples. In other words, because He gives to us, we give freely to others.

In Matthew 5:16 it says, *"...let your light shine before others, so that they may see your good works, and give glory to your Father in Heaven."* Let you light shine in all that you do so that God will be honored. In his book *The Prayer That God Answers*, Dr. Michael Youssef says that we do not honor God when we give with a *"fanfare and a press release."* Further, we do not honor God when we limit our giving to a small tithe in the collection plate. We honor God when we combine all of our actions and small tithes with the spiritual gifts that we have received, which are love, joy, peace, patience, kindness, goodness, faithfulness, gentleness and self-control.

Take a moment now to praise God for His spiritual gifts. Let His Spirit have complete control through your giving so that all honor is to God.

Week Two - Day Four
Honor in Receiving

Think for a moment about a gift that you purchased where you could hardly wait to see the joy on the face of the recipient. The first gift that I can remember giving was a 25-cent can opener for my mother. She received the gift as if it were a crown of glory given in recognition for the hundreds of meals prepared for our family of five. This was the response that I had anticipated. Not only had I honored her with my gift of love, but I watched as she honored me by using the gift.

How can we honor God in receiving? To the believer or nonbeliever, God's love is free. The only way to receive his love is by faith as did Jesus, Moses, Sarah, Mary, the twelve disciples and thousands more. This free gift of love is not like other gifts that might wear out or go out of style. It is an everlasting gift that includes forgiveness (Acts 26:18), abundance of grace (Romans 5:17), and the gifts of the Holy Spirit (Acts 2:38).

> *"I know what it is to have little, and I know what it is to have plenty. In any and all circumstances I have learned the secret of being well-fed and going hungry, of having plenty and being in need. I can do all things through Him who strengthens me"* (Philippians 4: 12-13).

Paul, in writing to the people of Philippi, points to the fact that he knows by experience what it is like to have much and be able to give to others, as well as what it is like to have little and have to rely on receiving from others. The secret, says Paul, is in our faith in God. *"I can do all things through Him who strengthens me."* **You must believe**

to receive. There are many believers who hear sermons, read the scriptures, memorize verses of scripture, volunteer for church service and may even have perfect church attendance, yet they are void of the fullness of God's love. Why? Because their life is not led by God. Somewhere along life's path, they have returned to their own way of thinking. They are going through the motions without truly receiving all that God has to give. What our churches need today are members who receive God's love daily as humble yet empowered believers, and then respond to His gift of love in service to others.

To believe in God and receive his love is uniquely personal. For some it might be triggered by a life and death situation or the experience of witnessing a miracle. It may by a simple moment of quiet realization of God's presence. To all it is a thought-altering experience that leads us to praise God. We praise God by receiving his love, and then because it is *"more blessed to give then receive"* (Acts 20:35), we share what we have received with others.

Take a moment to be still and receive His active power.
Now read John 1:12.

Week Two - Day Five
Honor Through Discipline

"Now discipline always seems painful rather than pleasant at the time, but later it yields the peaceful fruit of righteousness to those who have been trained by it" (Hebrews 12:11).

Spiritual discipline in love could be called the only calling of God. Without it we would be left to a discipline of our own human nature. There are myriads of disciplines referred to in the Bible, so where do we start? We do not start with a self discipline of our own making. In his book, *New Seed of Contemplation*, Thomas Merton writes, "There is no substance under the things which I am clothed. I am hollow...and when they are gone there will be nothing left of me but my own nakedness and emptiness and hollowness, to tell me that I am my own mistake."

We are indeed our own mistake with our self-imposed list of disciplines that increase daily. To honor and praise God though discipline is to exercise obedience to God. Matthew would have our spiritual discipline begin with seeking the kingdom of God and His righteousness (Matthew 6:33). This is not a kingdom that takes place in a distant future but a kingdom that is within each believer. Jesus said that it is by the *"finger of God"* (God's Spirit) that he cast out demons, and if this be so *"then the Kingdom of God has come to you"* (Luke 11:20). Again in the Lord's Prayer Jesus taught us to pray, *"...Thy Kingdom come, Thy will be done on earth..."* W.R.F. Browning suggests that the believer continues in active testimony of this discipline when he wrote, "The church (Christ's body) is the society which aims to keep the incentive and the attraction of the Kingdom." Matthew, Browning and Jesus understood that it is our discipline, in submission, that will open the gates of the kingdom to an outpouring of God's love.

We honor and praise God through discipline by seeking the discipline of His Spirit as did Jesus, Sojourner Truth, Billy Graham, John Wesley, William Booth and thousands more. As mentioned yesterday, this is a mind-altering experience and not for the faint of heart. "Discipline always seems painful rather than pleasant at the time, but later it yields the peaceful fruit of righteousness to those who are trained by it." Therein lies the key, *"trained by it."*

Think on these words today, *"...trained by it..."* and *"Seek ye first the Kingdom of God...."* They lead us to a spiritual discipline of love that results in honor and praise to God, and all other disciplines will then fall into their peaceful place of fruitfulness.

Week Two - Day Six
Honor Through Prayer

As humans our understanding of God is made up of dreamlike visions and childlike faith. We read and reread the Bible in hopes of understanding the purpose of our existence. Who is this God of love and what is the master plan for our life here on earth? We struggle to accept God and his love through limited human terms of understanding. It is no wonder that we have divisions in our churches; our Christian life is based on our own terms. There are a growing number of Christians who think that life is like preparing for a final exam where they must know all the answers or they will not receive a passing grade. The Bible teaches that we will never know all the answers to life, but we must live the answers that we know. So where do we get the answers? The answers come through a consistent connection with God known as prayer. To exclude prayer from our daily life will lead to self-interpretation of His love and we become part of, what I call, the "feel good" society. We choose a church that makes us *feel good* about Christianity, and we devour it whole. The question then becomes, where is our faith when we don't feel good? When we praise and honor God through prayer, it takes us into a wholeness that is far superior to a *feel good* mentality. Prayer is submission of weakness and power to the soul. Prayer takes us to an active expression of His love, which is for all seasons of life, summer, fall, winter and spring. It is prayer that equalizes all of our seasons so that our praise is in harmony with His love. **Prayer is our cycle of life.**

Praise and honor through prayer does not stop at the Father's ear. Prayer is our connection to God and His connection to us. As we lift our honor and praise to God in prayer, His Spirit penetrates our physical and mental being. When this happens, our prayer comes to life and we begin to live our prayer. We enter the prayer cycle of life and begin living the answers we know.

In his book, *The Prayer That God Answers*, Dr. Michael Youssef reminds us that "Living a life filled with praise allows real prayer to be launched. Such a life decentralizes the self."

In other words, when we focus on praise to God, our thoughts are turned away from our own selfish nature.

Today, I would like you to concentrate on listening to God. Open your mind and heart to Him in prayer and listen throughout the day to His response. The Holy Spirit will lead you in all situations. *"Be still and know that I am God!..."* (Psalm 46:10).

Week Two – Day Seven
Christian Life of Praise Through Honor

The word HONOR can mean many things. One can be honored for good works with medals, diplomas, special recognition dinners, etc. One can also pledge their honor as a promise, *On my honor I pledge...,* or as words of truth. *On my honor and hope to die, this is the truth,* etc.

The word honor conjures up various thoughts all of which are included in the life of a Christian.

The Christian life of praise through honor begins when we seek first the Kingdom of God and then allow the fruits of His Spirit to work through our life. Others will notice that our words of truth and love are not separate from our actions but joined as a unit in honor to God.

"Praise the Lord all you nations! Extol Him all you peoples! For great is His steadfast Love toward us, and the fruitfulness of the Lord endures forever. Praise the Lord!" (Psalm 117).

Week Three – Day One
Praise Through Worship

Paul is very specific about worship as recorded in Acts 17: 22-31. Read this scripture and then write a short paragraph about Paul's message of worship.

It is essential, for our daily spiritual growth to honor God in teaching, giving, receiving, prayer and discipline. These things are a by-product of true worship, for it is by HONOR that we are trained and through WORSHIP that God leads.

Jesus was trained in all manner of outward respect, which earlier we called honor, but it was His praise through worship that shaped His life as a living vessel, filled to an overflow, with the fullness of love. In addition, Matthew, Mark, Luke, John, Peter, James and many others all knew a depth of worship that filled their lives with a controlling love and took them beyond their human self. In the verses that you read, Paul says, *"For in Him we live and move and have our being...."* Is this worship? If so, then what must we do to get there? *"Present your bodies as a living sacrifice, holy and acceptable to God which is your spiritual worship"* (Romans 12:1).

In this week's study we will touch on a few biblical teachings such as reverence, devotion, song, spirit and truth. All find their center in worship. Start this week thinking about your praise through worship, your "living sacrifice" to God. As you do, remember the words of Jesus, *"...worship the Lord your God, and serve Him only!"* (Matthew 4:10b).

Week Three – Day Two
Worship in Reverence

"Therefore, since we are receiving a Kingdom that cannot be shaken, let us give thanks, by which we offer to God an acceptable worship with reverence and awe. (Hebrews 12:28)

The printed words of the Bible are one form of human understanding where God can, and does, speak to the mind and soul of all mankind. Its writers were inspired by God to write about the beginning and ending of life and all that goes in between. Their writings include word pictures of bloodshed and crucifixion, angels in white, large stones, tiny mustard seeds, birds, beasts, sheep, love and hate. Their reverence for God is truly mixed with love and awe. Look around you and then write some word pictures of your life.

As I sit here, I see my computer and the telephone on my desk. I hear birds chirping and cars driving by and I realize that our human reverence for God is shaped by what we see and hear. These are word pictures and sounds that transfer to our mind and dictate how we praise and worship God. Amidst this mind and thought shaping, God speaks to each individual by leading us to see and hear his gifts of love, comfort, rest and peace. These are gifts that are beyond our human ability to create. When we limit our reverence to God solely on our human abilities, we find ourselves in a form of idol worship. We boast, brag and thrive on our accomplishments. Our walls and mantels become covered with certificates and trophies that feed our self-idol worship.

I worked with a gal who claimed to be an atheist. Her belief was that we are in control of our own destiny. As she put it, "If we are weak, it is because we have not done enough to nourish our mind and body. If we are in control of any situation, it is because we have made use of our own power and strength." She was a control freak, and her need for control touched all of her subordinates. Her reverence was to herself which left her limited to only that which she could create.

For the Christian there are no limits because *"In Him we live and move and have our being"* (Acts 17:28a). Think about that for a moment.

To praise and worship God through reverence is to believe that it is His almighty hand of love and power that leads us to His excellence. The badge of honor belongs to God, for he is the giver of all spiritual gifts. His spirit guides us to perfection of their use.

Look again at your life and surroundings. Is your praise through worship based on reverence for all that God has provided? For the Christian, it is in reverence that we thank God for the certificates on the wall and the trophies on the mantel. In reverence we praise and worship God for our unique gifts. In reverence we *"Ascribe to the Lord the glory due His name"* (I Chronicles 16:29a).

Week Three – Day Three
Worship Through Expressed Reverence

As stated yesterday, reverence is the belief that it is God's almighty hand of love and power that has led us to excellence. Today we expand that thought to an expressed reverence where we take action to bear witness to God with hope to accomplish His purpose of love for all mankind.

At first, Christian reverence for God is internal; the mind and spirit are convinced of His love. Second, we confess our sins to God and third, we express reverence to God through words and deeds. *"For one believes with the heart and so is justified, and one confesses with mouth and so is saved"* (Romans 10:10).

Remember the story of the little engine that said, "I think I can, I think I can"? Not only did the little engine think it could, but the story says that eventually it accomplished its goal. Our worship through reverence is much the same. We first believe in our mind, and the action that follows lifts our soul to a new level of reverence which is an expressed reverence.

When our eyes are turned upon Jesus, the desire to express our reverence is overwhelming. Our belief is changed from *I think I can* to *I know I can* and our expressed reverence takes action. God's love is now working through our life and actions; we are His expressed reverence.

In a song by Helen H. Lemmel, she says, "Turn your eyes upon Jesus, look full in His wonderful face, and the things of earth will grow strangely dim, in the light of His glory and grace." You may be shy at first about verbalizing your love for God, but in time your spiritual growth will be difficult to contain. Turn your eyes upon Jesus daily and let His Spirit take control. The things of earth, and even your shyness, will grow dim in the light of His glory and grace. This is when our worship through expressed reverence begins.

The lesson today is powerful. Meditate on the fullness of its meaning in your walk with God.

Week Three - Day Four
Worship in Devotion

Devotion can be seen in many behavioral patterns of the children of God. Some of those patterns include religious intensity, striving to the utmost to please God and being zealous followers of the Word. These same patterns can be found in the nonbeliever with their intensity, striving to the utmost and zealousness toward crime, deceit and self. The difference is the motivation for the devotion.

> *"For where your treasure is, there your heart will be also"*
> (Matthew 6:21).

Many overtime hours have been spent to earn enough money to purchase some of the niceties of life such as a boat, car, remodeling of the house, etc. Some people are driven to purchase an infinity of stuff, far more than the few essentials actually needed to survive. There is nothing wrong with owning a car or boat or remodeling our house. God wants us to enjoy our human existence to the extent that we do not neglect our devotion to Him. To praise and worship in devotion is to serve one Master, and faith is the key that will open the door to true devotion. *"Faith is the assurance of things hoped for, the conviction of things not seen...By faith we understand that the worlds were prepared by the word of God, so that what is seen was made from things that are not visible"* (Hebrews 11:1 & 3). It is by faith, and faith only, that our devotion is firm in God. By faith we are convinced of His love, and thus we experience a positive new nature.

Faith, to some, is illusory. Their faith is based on an illusion of some miraculous self power to move mountains and heal the sick. But faith does not give us power; faith connects us to the power. We should not base our devotion to God on the result of our abilities but rather on faith in God's power to work in and through our life.

In our churches today there are many loving servants who are truly devoted to God. Unfortunately, there are many "would be" devoted servants who live to show off their self-inflicted wounds. You know the ones, those who are constantly letting all know about the amount of time that they have given to the church. They who scratch and claw their way to the highest positions of the church, giving all glory to themselves with little or no recognition to God.

My prayer is that all Christians would turn away from self devotion to a true devotion to God. *"No one can serve two masters..."* (Matthew 6:24).

Week Three – Day Five
Worship in Song

"Be exalted, O Lord, in your strength! We will sing and praise your power" (Psalm 21:13).

David sang praises in the form of Psalms which were about prayer, the Sabbath, the afflicted, praise, deliverance, lamenting, soul searching and many other topics. He also shared his Psalms with many choir directors. We don't know whether or not he was a great singer, but it is apparent that he knew the power of singing inspired words.

Think for a moment about your spiritual life. What does God mean to you? Have you had trials and triumphs, valleys and mountains in your life? Write a short psalm about your spiritual life.

My grandmother was inspired by words and music that she found in the church hymnal. The following are excerpts from a poem that she wrote. She was concerned that our singing of praise to God was somewhat automatic and that our singing was no longer from a heart of joy.

It's the Way They Sing

What has happened to the singing in the good ole church today?
They never make the rafters ring as in the olden day.
They pinch their lips together so the sound can just squeak out.
I remember well such good ole songs as "Let the Joy Bells Ring"
And the "Hallelujah Chorus," then the preacher's yell out, "Sing!"
They never cared for do, re, mi's, but sang right from the heart.
They never left it up to one, but each would do his part.
They never called them amateurs or some professionals rare.
They shouted, "Everybody sing!" and it made you glad you's there.
Why not all of you just try it in the good ole-fashioned way,
And you'll feel a heap lot better 'cause you sang your best today.
I'll bet those same ole rafters will echo back at you.
And you'll find yourself a-singing mighty well before you're through.

~ Della M. Bowman ~

If you know the words and melody to the song "Praise God From Whom All Blessings Flow," silently, or aloud, sing it now.

> *"Praise God from whom all blessings flow.*
> *Praise Him all creatures here below.*
> *Praise Him above the Heavenly Host.*
> *Praise Father, Son and Holy Ghost."*

Lest you think that you are not a good singer, I suggest that God will sing through you. Maybe not in audible tones but His Spirit within will cause your life to sing praises in everything that you do and say. Go back to the first line of my grandmother's poem. Change it to read *"What has happened to the singing from the soul in the good ole church today?"* The poem now becomes an invitation to live a life to sing about in our soul.

Let go and let God sing through you. Praise Him with your song of life. I guarantee that you'll feel *mighty well before you're through.* Say a prayer that your life will worship God in song today and every day.

"Let the word of Christ dwell in you richly, teach and admonish one another in all wisdom; and with gratitude in your hearts sing psalms, hymns, and spiritual songs to God" (Colossians 3:16).

Week Three – Day Six
Worship in Spirit and Truth

We have now passed the halfway point in this 5-week study on praise. Thus far we have studied about life's actions as an expression of God's love. The remainder of our study will be centered in the truth of Jesus's words:

"You did not choose me but I chose you..." (John 15:16a).

"But the hour is coming, and is now here, when the true worshipers will worship the Father in spirit and truth, for the Father seeks such as these to worship Him. God is spirit and those who worship Him must worship in spirit and truth" (John 4: 23-24).

What does it mean to worship God in spirit and truth? To worship in *spirit* is to praise God in the highest. This goes beyond giving praise in church or an outward display of good works. To worship in spirit is to abide in the belief that you are chosen by God. Jesus said that if we abide in him, he will direct our path. It will be a path that is chosen to be a part of the perfect body of Christ under the influence of the Holy Spirit. To praise and worship God in spirit is to abide in His love, period! Then the expression of His love through us becomes automatic, not contrived.

To worship God in *truth* is to live in sincerity and honesty based on what we know to be the truth of his love. There are many people who are loving and kind but go through life without accepting the truth of God's love. Unfortunately, when they die, the recipients of their loving kindness experience an emptiness that will never be regained. There is no hope for the future; the buck stops here.

The true worshiper lives in truth and praise to God. When he is gone, the recipients may experience an emptiness due to the loss of a loved one, but there is hope of eternal life.

How do we worship in *spirit* and *truth*? We abide in the life of Jesus. It was through His life and now through His spirit, the Comforter, that we are led to worship in spirit and truth.

Week Three – Day Seven
Worship in the Beauty of Holiness

"Give unto the Lord the glory due His name: Bring an offering and come before Him; Worship the Lord in the beauty of holiness" (I Chronicles 16:29 KJV).

Holiness seems to be a dividing line, a mystery, for some Christians. Yet our praise and worship of God through reverence, devotion, song, spirit and truth are all inclusive in the beauty of holiness. Write below what the beauty of holiness means to you:

The holiness of God would seem to separate us from God because, in fact, His holiness is far superior to us. However, if we consider our spiritual function as a part of the body of Christ, then there is no separation. What does this mean? Am I God? No, neither you or I are

God, but this does not diminish the fact that God does share His holiness with believers. We are one in His love and the unique gifts of His Spirit.

Read Psalm 145 and notice the progression:

1) God's sovereignty as the only Holy God.

2) God's Holiness shared with those who believe.

3) The desire of the believer to proclaim the beauty of His holiness.

It is evident that all the writers of the Bible agree with the Psalmist that there is only one true God who does share His holiness with all believers. In truth, the meaning of the Hebrew words for holy and holiness is separation, but this separation is not from God. It is a separation from sin, and as such, we are holy as God is holy. To worship in the beauty of holiness is to live a life of praise to God for our separation from sin.

A newborn baby learns that if he cries he will be fed. He soon learns how to come to the table and feed himself. As an adult, his early training comes to fruition as he nourishes himself daily. It is much the same when we live a life in the beauty of holiness. Our daily training by God to stand separate and holy, as He is holy, comes to fruition through daily nourishment and we grow in His love. We are more than conquerors through Jesus Christ. We are dead to sin (the penalty is removed) and alive unto God (His holiness is ours). Christ's death and resurrection becomes our death and resurrection: the death of the old self and the resurrection of the new self. This is the beauty of holiness.

Week Four - Day One
Praise Through Prayer

What is prayer? The dictionary simply states that prayer is an earnest request; the act of practice of addressing a Divinity, especially in petition. The Bible teaches that prayer is much more than an "earnest request." It is a submission in faith to the omnipotence of God and praise for His power and love.

In his book *Pray the Price*, Dr. Terry Teykl states, "...our churches may have an inspired vision, abundant resources and a good location...yet, without prayer we are left at the mercy of every religious fad or trend." It is indeed prayer that keeps us on the spiritual path of life. Prayer is essential to the life of the Christian and should be number one on our life's agenda. I am not talking about a prayer that is carefully worded so as to impress others, nor the prayer that is by rote or in some form of ritual that has lost its meaning to the one who is praying. The prayer that this week's study is centered around is the prayer to God that is in praise and submission to His authority and teaching.

I read a story about a woman who was invited to visit a friend's church. She was moved by the music and message and promised to visit again the following Sunday. During the week she found herself anticipating her next visit. She was not disappointed at her second visit and was moved again by the music and the message. But this visit was different. The pastor asked everyone to close their eyes and then he gave this invitation, "If you feel God speaking to you, raise your hand." Her hand went up so fast it surprised her. Then the pastor invited all who raised their hands to pray silently or aloud a prayer of praise to God for forgiveness of sin through Jesus Christ. This she did and in the days that followed, while her lifestyle never changed, she felt assured that she now lived with God's blessing. Several months into her conversion, she decided to learn how to pray as she had heard others pray. While taking a bath, she tried praying aloud and it felt good. Eventually her prayer time moved from the bathroom to the kitchen, and then to the car. Prayer was becoming a part of her life on a daily basis. She began to feel God's presence during her prayer time. Ideas would pop into her head during and after her prayer. God was speaking to her. Within the space of two years, her lifestyle was completely changed.

Prayer is our connection to God and His direct connection with us.

Prayer is the Christian's cycle of life.

The goal for this week is to learn that the prayer cycle of life is not one way. Yes, we pray to God in submission and praise, but our prayer should not end there. We must listen to God's response. In anticipation to this week's study about prayer, pray now this earnest request to God:

Dearest Father,
I praise your almighty power and love. I open my heart and mind to your leading. Not my will but Thine be done.
Amen.

Week Four – Day Two
Prayer Commitment

Communication is essential to all of God's creatures. We humans have even devised ways to communicate with the blind, deaf and vocally impaired. In my early 20s, I was the program director at a Salvation Army camp. The variety of outreach through the Army camps was a true challenge. There were camps for senior citizens, single moms and their children, scouts, the blind and the deaf. At one of the camps, we had a lady who was both blind and deaf. She had a guide with her who carried a small machine which looked like a tiny typewriter. For those of you who have never used a typewriter, it is similar to a computer keyboard. It had two sets of keys, one with the letters of the alphabet and the other with dots for typing in braille. At the top of the keyboard, there was a hole, about the size of the nail on your index finger, where she would place her finger. As I typed, a message was translated in braille to her finger. I would greet her every day through the use of this God-inspired invention aware of the fact that without it there would be little or no communication with this camper. More than once I thought of how hopeless her life would be without this means of communication.

So it is with the Christian. Without a means to communicate with God, our life is hopeless. We see and hear the beauty of His creation, but without communication we are left without a direction, a purpose, a hope.

In his life, Jesus gave us an example of true communication with the Father through daily prayer. So you might ask, is there a certain time or place that we should pray? The psalmist said, *"At noon I will pray."* Jeremiah said, *"Pray now to the Lord."* Matthew said, *"Go to your room and pray."* Paul said, *"we ought ourselves to continually pray"* and *"Pray without ceasing."* Peter prayed on a rooftop, and Jesus prayed in a garden, on a cross, in the daytime and at night. The Bible is not specific as to when or where we should pray, but it is very clear that our prayer commitment is an assignment for life and that God is always listening.

Your assignment today is to commit the day to constant prayer. Pray in the morning before every task or silently during a conversation. Be constant in your commitment to prayer. We will share this prayer commitment experience in class.

It is important to remember that the content of our prayer comes second to our commitment. Commitment to prayer is what Jesus taught his followers through words and actions.

"Blessed be God, because he has not rejected my prayer or removed his steadfast love from me" (Psalm 66:20).

Week Four – Day Three
Pray – To Whom?

"Pray in this way; Our Father in heaven, hallowed be your name..." (Matthew 6:9).

We are to pray to "Our Father," but who is our father? Our Father is not an earthly birth parent, a seasoned citizen of knowledge or an ancestor. Our Father is Lord, creator and guardian of all things (Genesis 1; Isaiah 64:8; I Corinthians 8:6); The God of miracles (John 3:2); The God of Salvation (Isaiah 12:2); The God of patience (Romans 15:5); Love and Peace (II Corinthians 13:11); Light (I John 1:5); Everlasting (Genesis 21:33) and Eternal (I Peter 5:10).

To whom do we pray? We pray to "Our Father." If we lose sight of the fact that we are praying in surrender to "Our Father" then our prayers become a mere selfish attempt to manipulate God's will to conform to our personal desire. Dr. Michael Youssef, in his book *The Prayer that God Answers*, has this to say about prayer: "We love to pray—if it's convenient. We love to pray—if it doesn't interfere with our busy lifestyle. We love to pray—if it doesn't get in the way of our Christian ministry. For, make no mistake, one of the principle blights of evangelical Christianity is our activism. We prefer doing to being; we value action over prayer. Yet prayer is what makes actions—our ministry—effective for God's purpose."

To whom do we pray? We pray to "Our Father" not for what He is capable of doing for us but to praise Him for what He can and will do through our life. We do not always receive what we want, but "Our Father" always gives us all that we need.

I received an e-mail which reads, in part:

> I asked for strength and God gave me difficulties to make me strong. I asked for wisdom and God gave me problems to solve. I asked for prosperity and God gave me a brain and strength to work. I asked for courage and God gave me danger to overcome. I asked for love and God gave me troubled people to help. I asked for favors and God gave me opportunities. I received nothing I wanted...I received everything I needed.

To whom do we pray? We pray to "Our Father" who will change our self-satisfaction, which is momentary, to a soul satisfaction which is eternal. And we pray in faith believing that "Our Father" is the supreme ruler of love and will guard all that we have committed to Him against evil. To whom do we pray? *After this manner therefore pray ye;* **Our Father** *which art in heaven*...

Week Four – Day Four
Pray in Faith

There are three elements of thought that should not be denied on our journey of praise through prayer in faith.

First, give God His rightful place with complete confidence. H. William Gregory states in his book, *Faith Before Faithfulness*, "Prayer dethrones the ego and puts God in God's rightful place: The center of our lives." Prayer is a discipline that must be active in the life of every Christian because without it the continuity of our spiritual growth is delayed. Without prayer we turn our faith away from God and place it in the power of our own ego. Jesus taught us to pray, "Our Father…Hallowed be Thy name…" When we pray in this way we give God His rightful place of authority.

Second, praise God in submission to His purpose for our existence. This is where the words of Hebrews 11:1 began to have meaning to our soul. *"Faith is the assurance of things hoped for, the conviction of things not seen."*

The two blind men (Matthew 9: 27-29) could not see Jesus, but they had heard about his miracles. They followed Jesus crying, "Have mercy on us." Jesus asked them if they believed and the men answered, *"Yes."* Jesus then acknowledged their faith and restored their sight. Their faith was not based on what they saw. They were blind, yet their cry to Jesus was a confident cry of faith, a submission to the power of Jesus. Most people zero in on the restoration of sight for these two men and overlook the act of submission in faith. The two men had a specific goal in mind as do many Christians when they come to Jesus in prayer, but the goal is insignificant to their story or even the prayer. What is significant is that the prayer is in submission to God's purpose for our existence. Submission to the power of God will take us beyond knowledge of accepting God's authority, to the wisdom of assurance/confidence that He has a purpose for our existence that is far greater then any goal that we have in mind. **Submissive faith changes lives forever.**

Third, praise God for all personal experiences. Faith is no stranger to challenges, especially in the areas of patience and endurance, yet it allows us confidence in God's time. Noah's faith gave him patience and endurance while in the ark. Abraham and Sarah waited almost a lifetime for the birth of their first child. Peter fished all day without catching any fish. What thoughts might have entered their minds? Was Noah getting impatient when he sent out the raven and then the dove to check if the water had subsided? Did he think that God was taking too long with this flood? Had Abraham and Sarah resigned themselves to the thought that God was never going to answer their prayers for a child? Did Peter give up on fishing with the thought that God did not favor him on that day? We all have a tendency to want God to fit into our important and valuable time frame. We want healing, financial assistance and answers *now!*

Let's look back to a few generations ago when they had to wait 5-10 minutes for their coffee to brew and they had a toaster that toasted one side of the bread at a time. They had no television or computers and there was one telephone per household. What progress has been made and all in favor of faster communication and saving time. We have come to rely on the 2-minute coffee maker and cell phones, etc. to the point that we expect God to fit into our time frame. Perhaps the greatest lesson of this entire study is to **pray in faith**, confident that our existence has a purpose and that God will guide us in His time and His way.

HOPE is the desire for fulfillment. FAITH is the confidence that the fulfillment will take place.

Week Four – Day Five
Pray for Others

My prayers for others are usually centered around my family and close friends. On occasion I expand my prayers to include whole groups of people like those who are suffering from famine and earthquakes or those caught in the midst of war. Then there was the time when I was angry with God. I reminded God of His promise in John 14:13. *"I will do whatever you ask in my name, so that the Father may be glorified in the Son."* This prayer was very personal because my infant great-niece was in desperate need of a liver transplant. The doctor said that a liver must be found within two months or Amber would die. I have prayed many times and not received an answer to my prayer, but this time I was not going to take NO for an answer. I wonder if God was amused at my demand? He certainly understood my sincerity in faith. Now as I reflect on this event, I have a new understanding of His grace. Yes, Amber did get her transplant and is now 13 years old.

Here is how the miracle worked. God used a grandmother (my sister), a newspaper reporter, a television news anchor, a state senator, a TV program about organ donation and an 11-year-old girl named Victoria Lord. God also listened to the prayers of hundreds of people, including those of my own congregation, and a miracle happened. The donor 11-year-old Victoria, after watching a program about organ donation, turned to her parents and told them that when she died she wanted to donate her organs. I believe that it was at this moment that God knew that little Victoria was ready to come home to Him. She was willing to die to save another and God took her into His loving arms.

I am telling you this story because of the last part of the verse that I quoted earlier where Jesus said, *"...that the Father may be glorified in the Son."* I understand now that our prayers will be answered if the end result will glorify God rather than satisfy a selfish desire. What if Amber had not received a liver transplant? What words would I have written? I honestly don't know, but of this I am certain, I have been spiritually changed because of this event in my life. Not because Amber lives, but because little Victoria was willing to die to save another. I am beginning to understand in my soul what I have always known in my mind, the love behind the death of Jesus who was willing to die for all mankind.

The Bible teaches that the power of prayer extends beyond our initial request because God has no limits. In the case of my great-niece Amber, prayer reached out to a grandmother, a reporter, a TV news anchor, a state senator and now to all of you who have read this story. The prayer remains active and continues to glorify God.

There is one more thought about our prayers for others which is often overlooked and that is to follow our prayers by telling others that we are praying for them. Jesus followed his prayer for Simon by telling him, *"...I have prayed for you that your own faith may not fail"* (Luke 22:32). Paul, when writing to the people of Colossae, said, *"...we have not ceased praying for you..."* (Colossians 1:9). As you praise God in prayer for others, think about extending the action of your prayer. This can be done through a phone call, letter or short note to a loved one, friend, soldier, missionary, the President, a senator, etc. telling them that you are praying for them.

Our special commission from Jesus is that when we pray for others, the end result will glorify God and keep our prayers active beyond the final amen.

Week Four – Day Six
Pray for Healing

True healing is the restoration of our spirit so that we are again in the image of God; not a physical image but a spiritual image of love that flows through our physical being.

This healing of our spirit takes place though the death of Jesus and our acceptance of this gift of love. Once our spirit is healed, we are faced with the reality that our spirit is living in a human body that is subject to pain and suffering. Should we then pray for healing when we know that it is inevitable that the human body will suffer pain? If we look to the life of Jesus, the answer is yes. He not only prayed for others, but he prayed for himself when he asked for the cup (the pain) to be passed from him. One of the most important lessons from the life of Jesus is that prayer is an outreach of the believer's faith:

1) Faith that God hears our prayer.
2) Faith in submission to the will of the Father, and
3) Faith, whether physical healing occurs or not,
    that in all circumstances our Father will be glorified.

The disciples saw that Jesus gained strength and direction when he prayed, so they asked Jesus to teach them to pray. They wanted to be more like Jesus in spiritual strength and healing powers. Can you imagine their amazement when Jesus said to them, "*...the one who believes in me will also do the works that I do and , in fact, will do greater works than these...*" (John 14:12). Jesus taught them that faith in Him should always come first. What follows is the prayer in faith, which produces all miracles of strength and healing.

In our churches today we have lost the message of the power of prayer in faith. We are stuck on HOPE of the fulfillment never going beyond to FAITH that the fulfillment will take place. Having said that, I do not know why, after much prayer, some are physically healed and others are not. What I do know is that Christians, even in suffering have spiritual strength and healing of the soul, a fulfillment that enables them to endure.

My mother, while in her teens, lost her grandfather, father and her 11-year-old brother, all within six months. Today at age 90 with her loss of physical activity due to arthritis and her failing eyesight and the mental impairment of dementia, she continues to sing over and over again, *"God will take care of you (me), through every day, o'er all the way..."* You see, she has learned the prayer of faith, which has eternally healed her soul.

Prayer in faith does produce miracles of physical healing, and perhaps more importantly, it affords the miracle of endurance through the joy in suffering. If we are to follow the example of Jesus, we must be vigilant in our prayer of faith for healing of the body and soul.

Week Four – Day Seven
Living in the Power of Prayer

"For the kingdom of God depends not on talk but on power" (I Corinthians 4:20).

We have thousands of churches with wonderful activities that satisfy the self interests of its people. Where is the praise and power? Many congregations are growing into the hundreds, yet they are lacking in praise and power. As Dr. Youssef says, "Who turned the power off?" Think about your church. Is the power on or off? Our faith-based prayer to God, who is our source of spiritual power, is the only way to turn the power back on. *"All things can be done for the one who believes"* (Mark 9:23).

Remember in the "cycle of life" our praise through prayer keeps us connected to God's Spirit which produces a witness of the Power of God.

Effective prayer is believing, not wondering.

Week Five – Day One
Love

Thus far, our concept of praise has been somewhat definitive. We began with praise as an *expressed approval* of a good deed and progressed to praise of anticipation for God's active power through our life. We then highlighted our praise in action through honor, worship and prayer. This final week will bring us full cycle back to the cause of praise, which is love, God's embrace.

> *"In the beginning was the Word, and the Word was with God, and the Word was God...And the Word became flesh and lived among us..."* (John 1: 1& 14a).

We are fascinated with photos, writings and film documentaries about the history of our country. They help us to understand and appreciate the struggles and joy that took place in the making of this great nation. Excitement mounts when we place one of our relatives in an active role in our nation's history. I have the documentation for two members of my family who had a small part in the history of our nation. The first is an ancestor who was a soldier in the American Revolutionary War. The second is my mother who played in the 1935 World Series of Amateur Softball. (Her team lost to the Bloomer Girls of Cleveland.) With all of this love for history, why is it that so few have read the Bible? It has great documentation with first-hand accounts of war, murder, deceit, sex, love and miracles. There are poems, songs, visions, prophecies and even a promise of eternal life. So why have so few read the Bible? I suggest the following:

1) The Bible is a difficult read because its written form is from a different time in history.
2) There is a common belief that the Bible was written only for Christians.
3) It is easier to sit back and listen to someone preach their interpretation of the Bible rather than read it on their own.

It has been said that our Christian example may be the only Bible that some people read. Jesus understood the truth of these words. His knowledge of the written Word was put into motion as the living Word so that by example He taught all Christians to live in the image of His love. Too many good people fall short of this teaching. They read and reread the Bible and even commit some of the verses to memory but fail to grasp the connection of affection that is designed to flow from God through their life as an example of His love.

> *"So God created humankind in His image, in the image of God He created them; male and female..."* (Genesis 1:27). We are all created in the image of His love. Our bookshelves may be lined with Bibles of every interpretation but without love we are nothing. *"...If I have prophetic powers, and understanding all mysteries and all knowledge, and if I have all faith, so as to remove mountains, but do not have love, I am nothing"* (I Corinthians 13:2).

Love, the embrace of God, is found in the heavens, earth, wind, water, light, darkness, vegetation, trees, every living creature on land, in the water and in the air. Love, the embrace of God, is also found in the words of the Bible and through the life and death of Jesus Christ. It continues through our Christian example. Could it be that others are not drawn to His embrace of love because they do not see that embrace in our life?

Today, pay particular attention to your conversations and actions. Do others see in you love, God's embrace?

Week Five – Day Two
Accepting the Embrace

"We love because He first loved us" (I John 4:19).

It is easy to accept the hugs and kisses of a small child. Their love is sincere, without motive and usually triggers an uncontrollable response of love in return. Take that same love and multiply it to the nth degree and you have the embrace of God. Accepting this embrace starts on the inside and radiates outward.

The people of Shinar (Genesis 11) set out to *"make a name for ourselves"* by building *"a tower with its top in the heavens."* Today we see many churches building new additions that are simply all show and no go. Their purpose is to make a name for themselves, but their efforts are hollow. The modeling and remodeling of our churches must be from the inside where, by faith, we accept the embrace of love. Then the radiance of that love will, like the hugs and kisses of a child, bring warmth to others. Christianity is not a show-off sport where the Christian gains recognition by his actions. Christianity is accepting the embrace of God and giving Him all the glory.

Take some time this week and let God speak through you, share your testimony with a friend.

Week Five – Day Three
Understanding the Embrace

Without looking back to the first two days of this week, write a paragraph about 1) the embrace of God and 2) how God embraces your life.

If you find #2 difficult to write about, start carrying a notebook with you and write down the times that you feel His presence. It may be in the warmth of a sunlit day, the touch of a child's hand or an unexpected "thank you" from your boss. Tune your eyes and ears to your surroundings and you will be happily surprised at the evidence of God's daily embrace. We can quiet ourselves for a few moments of devotion each day; this is good, yet our understanding of God's embrace is widened when we realize that God is with us at all times.

We do not enter school at age 5 and start learning about verbs and the complexities of advanced mathematics. No, we start with basic learning skills and from there we build to another level of understanding. Our walk with God is very similar in that we are given enough understanding for each day and from this we develop spiritual wisdom. God's love is sufficient for today.

Understanding the embrace comes through the experience of living in His love. We cannot create this love. True love has always been and will always be the property of God. We can be good people and give the appearance of being a loving person, but this falls short of living in God's love, more specifically, letting God live through your life.

Be conscious of his embrace today.

Week Five – Day Four
His Embrace Through Service

"Be ye doers of the word and not merely hearers..." (James 1:22).

This morning, one of the lead stories on the television was that the Mega Millions Lottery Jackpot is up to two hundred and eighty million dollars. I imagine that there are many Christians thinking about what they might do with that sum of money, perhaps even thinking that their service to God would be so much greater. The tithe to the church would be so satisfying not to mention all the good they could do to help the poor and needy. It is a sad but true fact that many people waste their time, energy and money toward dreams of this nature. Thoughts of doing good are not wrong, but the idea that something extraordinary must happen before we can truly serve God is very sad indeed. When we rely on material things or even other people for our strength or satisfaction, we are setting ourselves up for a big disappointment. I have seen congregations that literally live for every word, action and embrace of their pastor and when that pastor is transferred to another church or retires, the congregation begins to fall apart.

Our service to God, the church and others should not be dependent on money or our pastor or any thing other than God. **Our service** may be the reason that many churches are lacking in His fullness. What we need are people who live in **His service**. Jesus prayed (John 17), *"I have brought you glory on earth by completing the work that you gave me..."* It is not our service, but the service of God that we are equipped to complete.

"For, brethren. Ye have been called to liberty; only use not liberty for an occasion of the flesh, but by love serve one another" (Galatians 5:13 KJV).

List below some ways that we can extend the grace of God through service. We will refer to this later in the lesson.

Years ago I completed an American Red Cross training program on First Aid. The instructor told of a man who had just finished his training when he happened upon the scene of an accident. He eagerly jumped from his car, pushing through the crowd, and ran to the side of the victim. He took control of the scene and proceeded to use his newly learned skills in first aid. Then he heard a voice from the crowd say, "I'm a doctor. When you're ready for my help let me know." The man had forgotten one of the basic lessons of his training, which is to ask if there is a doctor present. In a somewhat similar way, this is what happens with many Christians. They have their Bible in hand as they rush to serve, but they fail to ask Jesus, the servant of all, to take control.

Now look at your list of service that you wrote earlier in this lesson. Is your list determined by what you think would be acceptable service, or is it a list of the leading of God in your life? Don't panic, I suspect that there is a little of both in everyone's list. At the bottom of your list write these words, TO BE DETERMINED. This is a reminder that our acts of service do not end when we turn off the lights and go to bed. When we allow God to serve through us, His love will continue in the minds and hearts of all those who we served today. We may never see the result of His service through our life, but we can be secure in the knowledge that we have completed His work for that day.

God desires that we simply abide in His love and allow Him to do the serving through us. We may collapse at night of exhaustion, but the fullness of His love will rejuvenate us again and again.

LOVING NOTE: Do not go any further in this study if you feel that you do not understand the doctrine of God's embrace living through your life in praise and love. Prayerfully return to Day One of this week remembering that we are saved by grace through faith.

"...By Grace you have been saved through faith, and this is not of your own doing, it is the gift of God" (Ephesians 2:8).

Week Five – Day Five
Returning the Embrace

What is a life of praise? There are many stories of men and women whose lives have been a testimony of praise to God, but can we, in a five-week study, answer the question *What is a life of praise?* We can list the attributes and character of people who have lived a life of praise. We can list Bible references of certain acts of praise like honor, worship and prayer. We can do all of the above, but we may never be able to define a life of praise because it is so unique to each individual.

Jesus taught that He is the vine, the source of all love and strength, and we are the branches that extend out to the world. The vine gives all talents and shape to the branches. This is God's praise to mankind. When we submit our life to God, we become the receivers of His love and unique praise through our special talents. If you are trying to emulate what you see in other Christians, you are limiting God's special gifts through your life.

> *"For as in one body we have many members and not all of the members have the same function, so we, who are many, are one body in Christ, and individually we are members one of another. We have gifts that differ according to the Grace given us..."* (Romans 12: 4-6a).

From this point on we will look at praise, not as an act of our doing, but as an act of God to all creation. Today, thank God for His praise through you in your function as a part of the body of Christ, a simple branch powered by His strength. Rejoice in your walk with God as you return the embrace through a life of His praise.

Week Five – Day Six
Accepting the Territory

For centuries prayers have been lifted to God for increased wisdom, comfort, spiritual vision and guidance. Indeed, the Bible teaches us to pray, but too many times our prayers come from a mind of uncertainty, loss or fear. It is as if we are testing God rather than coming to Him in faith. How many times must we have Jesus die on the cross? How many times do we demand proof of God's love? Jesus lived, died and was resurrected *once* for all mankind. His message is clear: *"I give you a new commandment, that you love one another. Just as I have loved you, you also should love one another. By this everyone will know that you are my disciples, if you have love for one another"* (John 13: 34-35).

We pray to God to increase our territory, but it is not the territory that needs to be increased, it is our faith and confidence in God. In Romans 8: 38-39 Paul gives one of the most confident and powerful testimonies of all time: *"For I am convinced that neither death, nor life, nor angels, nor rulers, nor things present, nor things to come, nor powers, nor height, nor depth, nor anything else in all creation will be able to separate us from the love of God in Christ Jesus our Lord."* The confidence expressed here is not unique to Paul. It is for all believers in Christ. Paul learned to turn his meditations to obedience and he began to see what God sees, a world of "territory" to show forth His praise.

"Ye are a chosen generation, a royal priesthood, a holy nation, a peculiar people, that ye should show forth the praises of Him who hath called you out of darkness into His marvelous light" (I Peter 2:9 KJV).

Because of God's praise to us we show forth the praises of Him. A win, win situation where we receive spiritual wisdom, vision and guidance to walk in *His* world, accepting *His* territory.

Take a moment to meditate on your life of praise with God.

"I will bless the Lord at all times; His praise shall continually be in my mouth. My soul makes its boast in the Lord; Let the humble hear and be glad. O magnify the Lord with me, and let us exalt His name together" (Psalm 34: 1-3).

Pray this prayer today:

Lord,
   Through your praise for me and in submission, I walk your territory today. I thank you that there are no limits or boundaries. Take my hand, precious Lord, and walk with me on your path of righteousness.
Amen

Week Five – Day Seven
Praise – the Lifestyle of Jesus

The Bible teaches that a perfect universe of love and harmony was created by God. Then God created man and woman in His image of love and gave them freedom to choose good or evil. When the human struggle ensued between good and evil, God continued to love. He inspired men to write of His love for all to read, yet the struggle continued. So God, in His great love, sent Jesus to live as an example of goodness for all to see. The *written* word now became the *living* word.

> *"And the word became flesh and lived among us, and we have seen His glory, the glory as of the Father's only son, full of grace and truth"* (John 1:14).

Every detail of the life of Jesus is not recorded in the Bible but what we do learn, through the lifestyle and teachings which are recorded, is that thousands were converted from a life of sin to a life of praise to God. His teaching was about the love of His Father for the people of all nations. To His followers he simply said *go and teach* this message to others. He taught, by example, to pray always. One of His prayers, recorded in John 17, shows us that he prayed not just for his disciples but for all future generations who hear the word of love. *"I ask not only on behalf of those* (the disciples)*, but also on behalf of those who will believe in me through their word* (future generations). God answered that prayer by blessing the disciples and generations of believers, past and present.

Jesus's entire life was consistent in praise to God through giving, receiving, discipline, prayer, reverence, commitment, service, obedience and above all in submission. He prayed with a confident faith that His Father would guide him to complete His mission on earth. More importantly, He lived A LIFE OF PRAISE.

You have now finished the 5 weeks of study about praise. My prayer is that His praise will permeate your entire being so that all who come near will feel the presence of God.

*"Finally, beloved, whatever is true, whatever is honorable, whatever is just, whatever is pure, whatever is pleasing, whatever is commendable, if there is any excellence and if there is any worth of **praise**, think about these things."* (Philippians 4:8)

Praise Be to God !

Psalm 23
A Psalm of Praise

The Lord is my shepherd—That's relationship!
I shall not want—That's supply!
He maketh me to lie down in green pastures—That's rest!
He leadeth me beside the still waters—That's refreshment!
He restoreth my soul—That's healing!
He leadeth me in the paths of righteousness—That's guidance!
For His name sake—That's purpose!
Yea, though I walk through the valley of the shadow of death—
    That's testing!
I will fear no evil—That's protection!
For thou art with me—That's faithfulness!
Thy rod and Thy staff they comfort me—That's discipline!
Thou prepares a table before me in the presence of mine enemies—
That's hope!
Thou annointest my head with oil—That's consecration!
My cup runneth over—That's abundance!
Surely goodness and mercy shall follow me all the days of my life—
That's blessing!
And I will dwell in the house of the Lord—That's security!
Forever—That's eternity!

Study/Discussion Notes

Week One: Praise 101
1) When we praise God, is our praise in expectation?
2) Is praise the result of things/events that are in our favor?
3) Read First Samuel 1: 10-11; 26-28 & 2: 1-2. What do Hannah's prayer and subsequent actions teach us about her praise?
4) What does "full effect" mean? (James 1: 2-4)

Week Two: Honor
1) Does an outward display of honor to God witness to the genuineness of our praise?
2) "...*By this time you ought to be teachers...*" In what way do these words challenge you?
3) What do you think that Jesus meant when he said, *"It is more blessed to give than to receive"* ? (Acts 2:35)
4) "Prayer, the cycle of life, equalizes all our seasons." What does this mean to you?

Week Three: Worship
1) Read Acts 17: 22-31. Discuss Paul's message to the heathen people about worship to false gods.
2) How do we arrive at reverence to God? (Hebrews 5:7)
3) Be prepared to shared the psalm that you were asked to write on day five of this week.

Week Four: Prayer
1) Share your experience of the assignment for prayer commitment on day two of this week.
2) How should we speak to God?
3) What does it mean to pray in faith?
4) What do the words "healing touch" mean to you?

Week Five: Love

1) You were given an assignment to be attentive during your conversations for one full day. Discuss the results.
2) Share your personal testimony in class.

Final Assignment

Compose a short statement about this 5-week study on praise.

Was it challenging? In what way and to what extent? Was it lacking in substance? In what way and to what extent? Mail your statement to:

Jacki K. Work
23717 Springbrook Dr.
Farmington Hills, MI 48336-2748

Let the first thing you say each morning brighten God's day.

Bibliography

1. YOUSSEF, MICHAEL - *The Prayer That God Answers*
Nashville, TN; Thomas Nelson Publisher.

2. MERTON, THOMAS - *New Seeds of Contemplation*
New York; New Directions, 1962.

3. LEMMEL, HELEN H. - *The United Methodist Hymnal*, 1989
The United Methodist Publishing House
40 Music Square E., Nashville, TN 37203.

4. TEYKL, TERRY - *Pray the Praise*
Muncie, IN; Prayer Point Press, 1997.

5. GREGORY, H. WILLIAM - *Faith Before Faithfulness*
Cleveland, OH; The Pilgrim Press, 1992.

Scripture quotations, unless indicated, are from The New
Revised Standard Version (NRSV) of the Bible, copyright
1989, by the Division of Christian Education of the National
Counsel of Christ in the United States of America.

Printed in the United States
29444LVS00005B/275